Dream Guitars
ILLUSTRATED

by MC Productions

ACKNOWLEDGMENTS

MC Productions wishes to thank everyone who helped to make *Dream Guitars Illustrated* a reality, as well as those who inspired and supported it:

Alice Dellavalle, Rita Sykes de la Pena, Greg Morgan, Tom Mulhern, Jay Scott, Steven Wilson, Music Sales Corporation, Ron Bienstock, James D'Aquisto, John Monteleone, Bob and Cindy Benedetto, Catherine Smith, Christine Read, Vic Da Pra, Albert Molinaro, Scott Chinery, Mike Carey, Stan Jay, Hap Kuffner, Lou Gatanas, John Santoro, Larry Wexer, Larry and James Acunto, Marc Horowitz, Robert Knippel, John Kinnemeyer, Meyer Rossabi, Fumi Nozawa, Peter Prisco, Sal Azzarelli, Ed Varuolo, Mark Simon, and all the great American guitar manufacturers whose legendary creations are honored in this publication.

Photos by Rita Sykes de la Rosa, Greg Morgan, John Bender Photography, and Gina Motisi
All guitar history text by Charles Dellavalle and Tom Mulhern

Order No. AM 92730
US International Standard Book Number: 0.8256.1451.1
UK International Standard Book Number: 0.7119.4826.7

Exclusive Distributors:
Music Sales Corporation
257 Park Avenue South, New York, NY 10003 USA
Music Sales Limited
8/9 Frith Street, London W1V 5TZ England
Music Sales Pty. Limited
120 Rothschild Street, Rosebery, Sydney, NSW 2018, Australia

Printed in the United States of America by
Vicks Lithograph and Printing Corporation

AMSCO PUBLICATIONS
New York • London • Paris • Sydney

Forwarding Appreciations...

Charlie has tirelessly taken on the task of capturing, on glossy paper, against pastel backgrounds, a phantasmagoria of ferry tisirable sextastrings. He has done all of this gathering of wonderful, even rare, fretted instruments, literally without leaving his studio, not unlike the way Sinatra is said to have recorded his *Duets* album. How, one may ask, can he have accomplished this with such elegance and panache? We know him, and can tell you that it was simply through contacts, perseverance, clean living, good taste, having high ceilings, and getting enough sleep. With the publication of this book, (whether he wants us to or not), we hold Charlie Dellavalle against the pastel backdrop of American Guitar History, and ensconce him in the pantheon of those who have devoted their lives to the Fretted Obsession.

Stan Jay
President, Mandolin Bros., Ltd.

I don't think that anybody who have ever had a love for vintage instruments stops buying, selling, collecting, or playing them. Many people cannot afford to collect vintage instruments or may only be able to buy one or two, but have that same passion and burning interest in the beauty and artistry that these instruments possess.

"A picture is worth a thousand words" is such an old quote that I don't know who to attribute it to. Charlie took a lot of time choosing and assembling the instruments for this project, so before I say a thousand words, maybe it's time for me to just say "Congratulations" and enjoy the pictures.

Hap Kuffner
Vintage Guitar Wholesaler/Exporter

The photos compiled by Charlie for this book are of some of the highest quality guitars ever produced. These instruments represent a standard of craftsmanship that hasn't existed in many years. These six string beauties will always hold a soft spot in my heart, as do the individuals who made them famous and invented what turned out to be the vintage guitar market.

Elvis pounding out chords on his Martin... John Lennon and his Rickenbacker on the Ed Sullivan Show... Jimmy Page and his '58 'Burst making us wear out our Led Zeppelin II albums learning his licks... Keith Richards open G tunings on his vintage Tele's... Jimi Hendrix letting us know that a Strat was made for more than just playing surf music. These are just a few individuals who helped vintage guitars get their start... Let's not forget our vintage roots!

Vic Da Pra
Guitar Collector/Historian/Author

The guitar is such an integral part of our culture. It has been at the foundation of social trends that have defined us. I have no doubt that the great guitars of the 19th and 20th centuries will transcend fine art in the 21st century. D'Aquistos and Martins will be the Picassos and Van Goghs to a new generation with wealth and a passion for the guitar.

Scott Chinery
Guitar Collector

When Charlie approached me with his idea of Classic American Guitar trading cards, I was very excited about the project. I thought it was unique and innovative and I told him that I welcomed the opportunity to share some of my Collectibles with other enthusiasts and collectors alike, and would be proud to be a part of it. The majority of the instruments depicted in the card sets are rare and are in excellent unmolested condition, and as we know, it is becoming increasingly more difficult on a daily basis to see and find guitars of this caliber. So his idea appealed to me on that level... and now, the beauty about presenting these instruments in a larger book format, showing even greater detail, color and clarity is very exciting... this is a must for anyone who appreciates quality.

Albert Molinaro
Guitars R Us, Los Angeles

CONTENTS

INTRODUCTION

Like six-string sugarplums dancing dolefully in the corner of Tiny Tim's little, addled eye, classic American guitars have been our sweetest dreams. 'Bones, 'bursts, dotnecks, slabboards, catseyes, pearltops: their nicknames alone have purged our daytime, desktop doldrums, cooled our fiercest fever dreams.

But now with the objects of our devotion almost priced out of our reach, only portraits of the past remain accessible, it seems. This book beautifully reprises the elegance, style, grace and scope of instruments that may have become mere dreams for most of us. As a large portion of our musical heritage passes quickly from our hands and our sweetest dreams give way to a waking, watchful reality we would perhaps have chosen not to see—to say nothing of abetting—this lovely book preserves our memories in photographs; it may soon be all that's left us.

Jay Scott
Guitar Historian/Author

1958 GIBSON FLYING V

s/n 8-2848

The original Gibson Flying V is easily one of the rarest solid-body electric guitars ever produced—or should we say underproduced! Gibson shipping totals show that only ninety-eight Flying Vs left the factory between 1958 and 1959, and there were even fewer of its sister guitar, the Explorer. With such a short supply and a high collector market demand, this African limba wood beauty (commonly referred to as *korina*) is one of the most costly as well. To complete this guitar-lover's fret dream is the original pink-lined brown case, hang tags, and strap.

Guitar courtesy of Albert Molinaro
Photo by Greg Morgan

1964 GIBSON FIREBIRD III

S/N 255523

Looking lovely and stylish, this Firebird III, one of only about 2,000 with the "reverse" body style, is a bold-looking guitar with some unusual features. Note the stud bridge with compensating ridges (as opposed to a Tune-o-matic design), Kluson banjo tuners, and a flatarm vibrato. Of the four original Firebird models offered by Gibson between 1963 and 1965, the Firebird III proved to be the most popular by showing the strongest shipping totals of the line. Custom colored Firebirds, regardless of model, are extremely rare. This custom shade is known as "Golden Mist."

Guitar courtesy of Meyer Rossabi
Photo by Rita Sykes de la Pena

1958 GIBSON EXPLORER

s/n 8-3882

This modernistic dream in its original brown rectangular case shares the title with the Flying V for the most collectible solid-body electric guitar. However, the Explorer also shared in the V's same initial dismal fate. Still a bit too radical in design for its time, only twenty-two original Explorers left the factory in 1958 and 1959. Some leftover Flying Vs and Explorers were released to the market in the early 1960s with '60s style appointments and are equally as rare. Despite its weak acceptance in the late '50s, Gibson has reissued this American classic successfully numerous times establishing it as one of rock's most respected axes.

Guitar courtesy of Albert Molinaro
Photo by Greg Morgan

1957 GIBSON LES PAUL STANDARD

S/N 7-6981

The Holy Grail? Well, at least one of them and in dead-mint condition (it still has its hang tags!). This Goldtop is simple elegance at its best with a tone to die for. Of special interest to collectors, this guitar is one of the original late '57 Standards to be fitted with "Patent Applied For" humbucking pickups. This is possibly the rarest Les Paul model configuration (and one of the best!) with low totals manufactured due to the introduction of the new Sunburst finish and the fact that many Goldtop Standards that year featured P-90 single coil pickups commonly referred to as "soapbars". A total of only 598 Les Paul Standards were produced in 1957.

Guitar courtesy of Chinery Collection
Photo by Rita Sykes de la Pena

1958 GIBSON LES PAUL STANDARD

S/N 8-6782

Proof that beauty is more than just skin-deep, this is the kind of guitar that makes you sigh—the way it looks and the way it sounds easily make it one of the most important solid-bodies ever made. The sunburst Les Paul Standard with a matched two-piece maple top debuted in mid '58 after the Goldtop was discontinued. Production total was approximately 1,700 between 1958 and 1960, making it a very rare and much in-demand piece. Originally selling for $265.00 with case, serious collectors will gladly pay 100 times that amount or more for a nicely figured "Burst."

Guitar courtesy of Lou Gatanas
Photo by Rita Sykes de la Pena

1951 FENDER TELECASTER

S/N 0067

The Telecaster is recognized as the first mass produced solid-body electric guitar, which allowed Leo Fender to pioneer an entirely new industry for electric instruments. Originally christened Broadcaster in 1950, Fender changed the name of their ground-breaking guitar to Telecaster in 1951. Since then, the Telecaster has been the guitar choice for many guitarists in just about every type of music. Early '50s "Black Guard" Teles (black Bakelite pickguard) are most revered by collectors for their tone and historical significance. This mint early example comes with its original form-fit case.

Guitar courtesy of Albert Molinaro
Photo by Greg Morgan

1951 FENDER PRECISION BASS

s/n 0386

In 1951, Leo Fender introduced an electric instrument that changed the sound of the rhythm section in American music forever. Not only was the Precision Bass the first electric bass guitar, it also featured a fretted fingerboard which allowed bass players to play their notes with accurate intonation and *precision*. From 1951 to the present day, extensive recording dates throughout American music history have featured the Fender Precision Bass earning it the undisputed title of "The Classic American Bass." Sporting the same butterscotch blonde finish and general appointments, this four-string wonder with its original vinyl gig bag makes a perfect companion to the previously featured 1951 Telecaster.

Guitar courtesy of Albert Molinaro
Photo by Greg Morgan

1957 FENDER PRECISION BASS

s/n 22938

By the late 1950s, the Fender Precision Bass had evolved into a significantly different instrument from the original pioneer bass guitar. New features included a "split" pickup, as well as an entirely new sculpted body style and headstock much like the popular Fender Stratocaster guitar. This beautiful example features an original anodized aluminum pickguard and is shown here with the original hang tags, case, and strap.

Guitar courtesy of Albert Molinaro
Photo by Greg Morgan

1954 FENDER STRATOCASTER

S/N 0105

Since its release in late 1954 to a somewhat skeptical music industry, the Stratocaster has become the most in-demand and highly visible guitar today. With its sleek contoured body, three pickups, and its revolutionary new tremolo bridge, the Stratocaster has withstood the test of time, making it one of the most versatile and design-worthy classics in guitar history. And speaking about test the of time, Lou Gatanas's dream guitar is one of the cleanest examples on the face of the planet. It is reported that a only few more than 100 Stratocasters left the Fender factory in 1954, which pretty much establishes this instrument as one for the museum.

Guitar courtesy of Lou Gatanas
Photo by Rita Sykes de la Pena

1958 FENDER "MARY KAYE" STRATOCASTER

S/N 34690

And while we're on the subject, here's the closest to Stratocaster heaven you're ever going to get! This beauty has an extremely rare blonde finish with gold-plated parts. Collectors have nicknamed it the "Mary Kaye" model after a Fender endorser who appeared in catalogs with these custom-colored guitars. Custom color Stratocasters were produced in extremely limited quantities during the '50s and the gold parts make this piece all the more rare. Even the buckle on its original strap is gold plated! Close inspection of this guitar reveals that the color is actually a blonde sunburst.

Guitar courtesy of Chinery Collection
Photo by Rita Sykes de la Pena

1963 FENDER BASS VI

S/N 92125

Yet another first for the Fender Guitar Company was the unique Bass VI. Tuned like a guitar only an octave lower, it allowed the guitarist to play or simulate a bass tone without having to get used to the larger scale Fender bass necks. The Bass VI shown here with its custom ordered "Champagne Pink Metal Flake" color is rare indeed! Production totals in general for these Fender dreams are tiny when compared with all the more popular models offered. Hats off to the person who custom ordered this back in the early 60s. It makes one wonder if he or she was aware of the rarity such a piece would become. Perhaps they were, since it remains in just about mint unplayed condition.

Guitar courtesy of Albert Molinaro
Photo by Greg Morgan

1966 FENDER JAGUAR

S/N L60858

Featuring the same new body design as its sister guitar, the Jazzmaster, the Fender Jaguar's main difference was a 24¾″ fingerboard scale length (like a Gibson) and two small single-coil pickups (unlike the larger Jazzmaster types). The Jaguar and the Jazzmaster were featured guitars during the early to mid '60s surf/beach party craze, and these Fender classics can be seen in action in just about any beach party movie from that era.

Guitar courstesy of Albert Molinaro
Photo by Greg Morgan

1935 RICKENBACHER ELECTRO SPANISH

S/N B452

In mid 1935, Adolph Rickenbacher (later spelled Rickenbacker) built the first solidbody electric Spanish guitar, with a decidedly new look: chrome and black Bakelite. Five decorative chromed plates cover hollow sections, and the huge "horseshoe" pickup also has a chromed cover. A powerful slide guitar, it didn't launch a solidbody revolution: It was up to Leo Fender's Broadcaster/Telecaster to do that in the early '50s.

This early electric guitar featured a detachable neck that the owner could easily replace should the original become worn or damaged.

Guitar courtesy of Mandolin Brothers
Photo by Rita Sykes de la Pena

1964 RICKENBACKER ELECTRIC 12 (Rose, Morris Export Model 1993)

S/N DL859

The shimmering tone of the Rickenbacker Electric twelve-string guitar was featured on numerous influential rock and pop hits of the 1960s. Only twenty-five "Rose, Morris Export Models" were made, and sport traditional *f*-holes instead of the unique Rickenbacker sound holes. Rose, Morris Ltd. was the British distribution agent for these Rickenbacker classics.

Guitar courtesy of Albert Molinaro
Photo by Greg Morgan

1963 NATIONAL GLENWOOD 98

s/n T64990

One need only observe the striking appearance of the National Glenwood to recognize its classic dream status. The fact that it was hollow, made of fiberglass, and offered in beautiful custom colors easily insured its place in American guitar history. These guitars produce a bright, singing tone especially suitable for bottleneck slide playing.

Guitar courtesy of Albert Molinaro
Photo by Greg Morgan

1931 NATIONAL STYLE O

S/N 52743

Before electricity and guitars became friends, the race for more volume led National's John Dopyera and his brothers (yes, their company was Dobro, which merged with National in 1932) to put an aluminum resonator cone inside of a metal-body guitar. Loud, yes, and certainly very honky-sounding. Great for slide, perfect for Hawaiian music. The nickel-plated brass body has a palm tree, mountain, beach, and clouds sandblasted into its top. Special praise must be given to this guitar's original owner for knitting a protective jacket for it when purchased new—thus preserving it in sparkling mint condition.

Guitar courtesy of Robert Knipple
Photo by Rita Sykes de la Pena

1941 MARTIN D-45

s/n 78630

The original prewar Martin D-45 with its extensive pearl inlays is the most elegant of flat-top acoustics. The first D-45 was manufactured in 1933 for country western movie star Gene Autry. In 1942, the Martin Company ceased production of this expensive model probably due to war restrictions and economy. During those nine years only ninety-one were produced. Finally in 1968, Martin proudly reissued this American classic, and it continues to be their flagship dreadnaught model to date.

Guitar courtesy of Albert Molinaro
Photo by Greg Morgan

1939 MARTIN D-28

S/N 72668

You're a bluegrass picker. You woke up one morning and this guitar is next to you. Obviously, you've died and gone to heaven! Only 123 D-28s were built in 1939, all with the distinctive herringbone trim, fourteen frets free of the body, and a big, room-filling tone that make this the most esteemed dreadnaught flat top acoustic ever.

Guitar courtesy of Marc Horowitz
Photo by Rita Sykes de la Pena

1951 D'ANGELICO NEW YORKER

S/N 1882

Although John D'Angelico only produced 1,164 guitars in his lifetime, they are the greatest of their kind. Every classic D'Angelico archtop guitar was made with such care and workmanship that they still continue to inspire guitar players, collectors, and builders worldwide. D'Angelico's handmade guitars are a unique blend of artistic taste with a tone and feel unparalleled at the time by factory-produced instruments.

Guitar courtesy of Albert Molinaro
Photo by Greg Morgan

1985 D'AQUISTO EXCEL

s/n 1182

Considered to be the greatest archtop builder of our time, James L. D'Aquisto built this superb hollow-body jazz guitar. James acquired and perfected his fine skill through his apprenticeship with friend and teacher John D'Angelico. After D'Angelico's death in 1964, D'Aquisto continued to build handmade guitars in the D'Angelico tradition. Throughout his career, James has incorporated new and innovative design ideas into his instruments giving them a unique appearance while never forsaking the workmanship and tone that set the standard for what a fine handmade guitar should be. Check out the awesome sunburst finish; supple, bound *f*-holes; and the exquisite ebony tailpiece. Fewer than fifty of these handcrafted jewels have been made.

Guitar courtesy of Larry Wexer
Photo by Rita Sykes de la Pena

1994 BENEDETTO RENAISSANCE SERIES IL FIORENTINO MODEL

S/N 31494

This exquisite masterpiece is the latest offering from world renowned violin and archtop guitar builder Robert Benedetto. Utilizing his skills as a fine violin maker, Benedetto has clearly gone beyond traditional archtop design. This 16″ wide noncutaway dream features twenty delicately cut clustered sound openings in its unbound European spruce top. The fingerboard, nut, and tailpiece are crafted from solid ebony, while the sculpted tuners and curly maple bridge are hand carved in classical violin making tradition. The delicate abalone inlay motif that graces the headstock, fingerboard, and body provides a simple, unadorned classic appearance. This is the first model in the Renaissance Series, and Bob already has plans for more.

Guitar courtesy of Robert Benedetto
Photo by John Bender Photography

1992 MONTELEONE RADIO CITY

S/N 145

Inspired by the classic art deco architecture of Manhattan in the 30s and 40s and by the world renowned Radio City Music Hall, John Monteleone has created an instrument that is the epitome of visual elegance. The headstock design alone, with its Radio City truss rod cover and spotlight inlays, takes one back to the glorious days of New York's golden jazz era. The guitar's beautiful inlays are made up of slender tapered wedges of mother of pearl and abalone shell arranged into geometric crystal patterns. But don't let the guitars stunning looks fool you. John Monteleone's guitars are extremely responsive to all forms of guitar techniques from heavy plectrum chord strumming to delicate fingerstyle melodies. This guitar is a true work of contemporary art that sounds amazing!

Guitar courtesy of John Monteleone
Photo by John Monteleone

1960 GIBSON SUPER 400 CN

S/N 14317

Super 400s first debuted in 1934, with a cutaway model introduced five years later. This carved-spruce-top model with curly maple sides and back has reigned supreme since then as one of the premier "big-box" jazz guitars. The Super 400 CN (cutaway, natural finish) shown here is one of only nine Super 400 CNs produced in 1960 and it's so clean, you'd swear it left the factory yesterday. What a dream!

Guitar courtesy of Mandolin Bros.
Photo by Rita Sykes de la Pena

1948 GIBSON L-5P

s/n 1320

Gibson's first postwar L-5 with a cutaway, the L-5P (*P* stands for Premier) was offered between 1947 and '48, with a name change to L-5C (for Cutaway) sometime in 1948. A total of only forty-four L-5 cutaway archtop guitars were shipped in 1948 and only forty-five in 1949. Like other L-5s, it was promoted as an orchestra model, meaning that it put out a lot of volume for an archtop acoustic—you wouldn't want the clarinets and saxes to drown you out, would you?

Guitar courtesy of John Santoro
Photo by Rita Sykes de la Pena

1948 GIBSON L-12P

S/N A1711

The *P* in this Gibson's name stood for Premier (in similar fashion to the previous L-5P), which meant that it was an early cutaway for this model. Actually, the L-12P was only made from 1947 through 1949, but with its gold-plated hardware, triple-bound top, and striking sunburst, it's still a beauty to behold half a century later. This guitar is one of 118 L-12 cutaway models to be shipped in 1948.

Guitar courtesy of Hap Kuffner
Photo by Rita Sykes de la Pena

1953 GIBSON SUPER 400 CES

S/N A15277

In 1951, a dozen years after it received its first cutaway, the Super 400 received a pair of pickups bringing this fantastic archtop into the electric age. One of sixteen produced in 1953, this example has two Alnico V pickups, an 18″ wide body, and so much class you feel like you should wear a tuxedo to play it. Compare this one with the acoustic Super 400 featured earlier.

Guitar courtesy of Mandolin Brothers
Photo by Rita Sykes de la Pena

1958 GIBSON ES 5 (SWITCHMASTER)

S/N A276674

The unusual combination of a 17″-wide L5 body shape with an arched maple top, a rosewood fingerboard, three pickups, six knobs, and an extra large pickup selector switch make the Gibson ES 5 Switchmaster featured here a visually stunning American classic. Approximately 450 Switchmasters were manufactured between 1955 and 1960, with the most desirable examples to collectors sporting three "Patent Applied For" humbucking pickups like the one shown here.

Guitar courtesy of Albert Molinaro
Photo by Greg Morgan

1968 TRINI LOPEZ DELUXE

s/n 523928

A popular entertainer/guitarist with a string of hits including "Lemon Tree" had his name attached to this rare (only 302 made!) full-depth '60s model. Its more popular counterpart, the Trini Lopez Standard, had rounded cutaways and a shallower body like an ES-335. The diamond soundholes; sharp, double body-cutaways; and Firebird headstock are extremely cool. Besides a pickup selector on the treble side, a standby switch is located on the bass side.

Guitar courtesy of Charles Dellavalle
Photo by Rita Sykes de la Pena

1959 EPIPHONE SHERATON MODEL E211N

S/N A3444

An early example of this rare semi-hollow-body electric made by Gibson using original Epiphone parts and pickups (Epiphone became part of Gibson in 1957), this Sheraton sports a Frequensator tailpiece, designed to improve the guitar's tone. Based on Gibson's successful ES-335 design, this guitar was the top of the semi-hollow Epiphone line. There were only three Sheratons manufactured in 1959 chosen to receive this beautiful natural blonde finish. Although all Sheratons are extremely rare, this has to be the most collectable example of this original first-year production model.

Guitar courtesy of Marc Horowitz
Photo by Rita Sykes de la Pena

1961 GIBSON ES 335

s/n 9856

Since its introduction in 1958, this dream guitar has remained the definitive blues machine due to its immediate acceptance by top blues and R&B performers, though musical history has shown that it is an extremely versatile guitar capable of any musical idiom. The 335 is an innovative guitar design primarily because it features a semi-hollow (solid center piece) body construction. This allowed guitarists to turn up the volume without full hollow-body feedback problems. Very early examples have an unbound rosewood fingerboard. The dot inlays were dropped in favor of larger rectangular inlays around 1962 or 1963.

Guitar courtesy of Albert Molinaro
Photo by Greg Morgan